AH-6
LITTLE BIRDS

BY CARLOS ALVAREZ

BELLWETHER MEDIA · MINNEAPOLIS, MN

Are you ready to take it to the extreme?
Torque books thrust you into the action-packed
world of sports, vehicles, and adventure. These books
may include dirt, smoke, fire, and dangerous stunts.
WARNING: read at your own risk.

Library of Congress Cataloging-in-Publication Data

Alvarez, Carlos, 1968-
AH-6 Little Birds / by Carlos Alvarez.
    p. cm. — (Torque: Military Machines)
  Includes bibliographical references and index.
  Summary: "Amazing photography accompanies engaging information about AH-6 Little Birds.
The combination of high-interest subject matter and light text is intended for students in grades 3
through 7"—Provided by publisher.
  ISBN 978-1-60014-578-0 (hardcover : alk. paper)
  1. Little Bird (Attack helicopter)—Juvenile literature. I. Title.
UG1232.A88A58 2011
623.74'63—dc22   2010034495

This edition first published in 2011 by Bellwether Media, Inc.

The images in this book are reproduced through the courtesy of: Boeing Image Gallery, front cover, p.
16; Ted Carlson/Fotodynamics, pp. 4-5, 6-7, 8-9, 13, 14-15, 18 (small), 20-21; Bob Ferguson/Boeing Image
Gallery, pp. 10-11; all other photos courtesy of the Department of Defense.

Printed in the United States of America, North Mankato, MN.
010111   1176

CONTENTS

THE AH-6 LITTLE BIRD IN ACTION

A steady rain is falling. Three AH-6 Little Birds fly low in the sky. They are on a **mission** to attack an enemy base. The advanced **sensors** of the Little Birds help the pilots **navigate** through the storm.

652

★ FAST FACT ★

The MH-6 Little Bird is similar to the AH-6. The MH-6's main missions are troop support and spying on enemies.

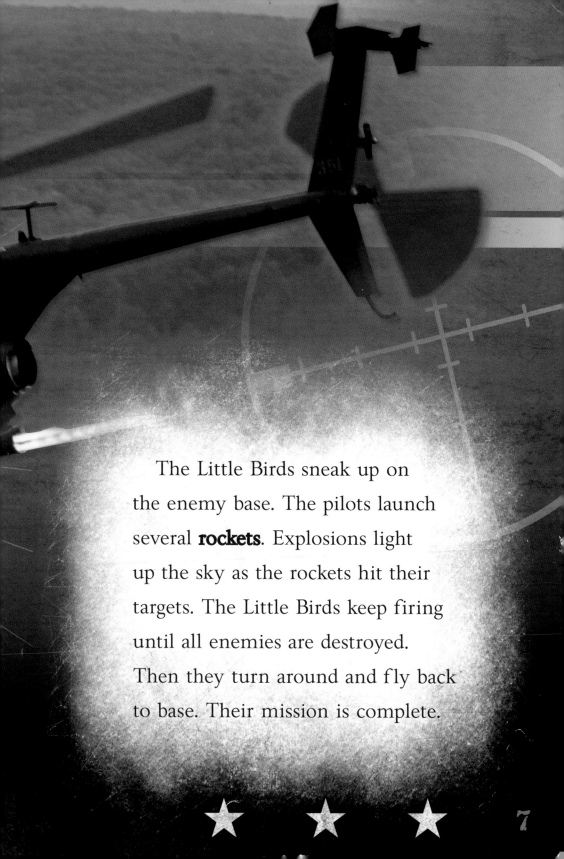

The Little Birds sneak up on the enemy base. The pilots launch several **rockets**. Explosions light up the sky as the rockets hit their targets. The Little Birds keep firing until all enemies are destroyed. Then they turn around and fly back to base. Their mission is complete.

LIGHT ATTACK HELICOPTER

The AH-6 Little Bird is a light attack helicopter. It is small, fast, and powerful. The AH-6's job is to find enemy targets, destroy them, and get back to base safely.

The Little Bird is mainly used by **special forces** of the United States Army. It is usually flown by the 160th Special Operations Aviation Regiment, or the Night Stalkers. The Night Stalkers provide **close air support** for other special operations units.

AH-6i

The AH-6i is a newer model of the Little Bird that has better sensors, more cockpit room, and better communications equipment.

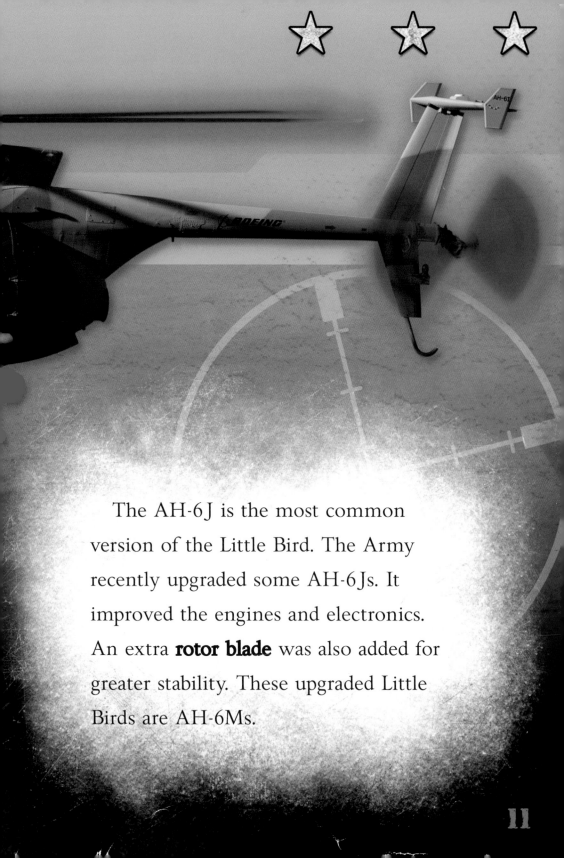

The AH-6J is the most common version of the Little Bird. The Army recently upgraded some AH-6Js. It improved the engines and electronics. An extra **rotor blade** was also added for greater stability. These upgraded Little Birds are AH-6Ms.

WEAPONS AND FEATURES

Little Birds can carry a wide range of weapons. They usually have two M134 **miniguns**. Each minigun has six barrels and can fire 4,000 rounds per minute. The Little Bird can also carry a GAU-19 machine gun. This gun fires 0.5-inch bullets from three barrels at a rate of either 1,000 or 2,000 rounds per minute.

M134 minigun

Many explosive weapons can be mounted to the Little Bird. One is the AGM-114 Hellfire guided **missile**. It can lock on to targets. The Little Bird can also fire rockets from M260 rocket launchers. Some missions require an Mk 19 **grenade launcher**. It can fire grenades at targets more than 1 mile (1.6 kilometers) away.

M260 rocket launcher

The Little Bird needs more than just weapons to perform its missions. Advanced **radar** helps pilots locate targets. The AH-6 also has a **forward-looking infrared (FLIR)** system that detects the heat of objects. This equipment helps pilots quickly locate and destroy enemy aircraft and vehicles.

forward-looking infrared (FLIR)

AH-6J
SPECIFICATIONS:

Primary Function: Light attack helicopter

Length: 32 feet, 2 inches (9.8 meters)

Height: 8 feet, 6 inches (2.6 meters)

Rotor Diameter: 26 feet, 7 inches (8.1 meters)

Maximum Weight: 3,550 pounds (1,610 kilograms)

Top Speed: 175 miles (282 kilometers) per hour

Ceiling: 16,000 feet (4,876 meters)

Range: 267 miles (430 kilometers)

Crew: 1-2

AH-6 MISSIONS

The AH-6 can fill many different roles for the U.S. Army. A single pilot can fly an AH-6. On some missions, a co-pilot is added to the crew. Little Bird pilots can perform missions during the day or at night. They can fly in almost any kind of weather.

Unmanned Little Bird (ULB)

The U.S. Army is planning to use a version of the AH-6 that can be flown without a pilot inside. The Unmanned Little Bird (ULB) will help keep pilots out of danger.

20

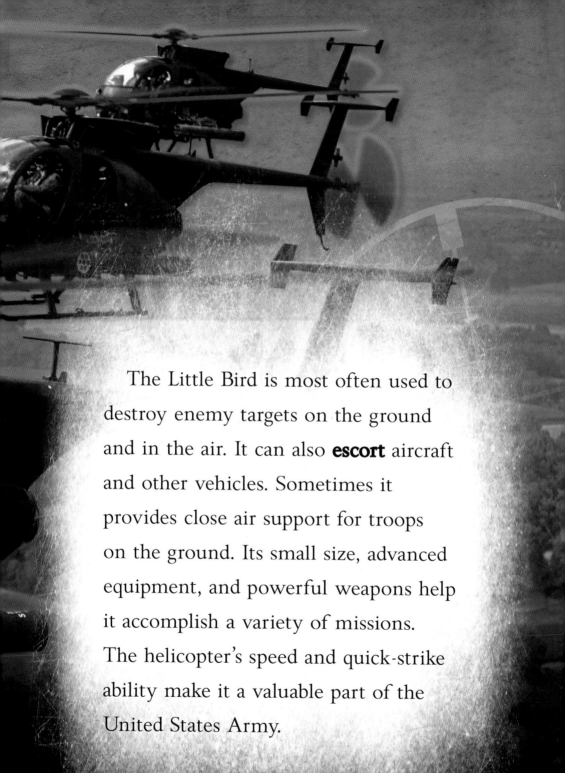

The Little Bird is most often used to destroy enemy targets on the ground and in the air. It can also **escort** aircraft and other vehicles. Sometimes it provides close air support for troops on the ground. Its small size, advanced equipment, and powerful weapons help it accomplish a variety of missions. The helicopter's speed and quick-strike ability make it a valuable part of the United States Army.

GLOSSARY

close air support—the role of supporting and protecting ground troops against enemy forces

escort—to travel alongside and protect

forward-looking infrared (FLIR)—a sensor system that uses the heat of objects to help pilots see in the dark

grenade launcher—a weapon that fires small explosives called grenades

miniguns—multi-barreled machine guns with very high rates of fire

missile—an explosive launched at targets on the ground or in the air

mission—a military task

navigate—to find one's way in unfamiliar terrain

radar—a sensor system that uses radio waves to locate objects in the air

rockets—flying explosives that are not guided

rotor blade—a blade on the rotor of a helicopter; the rotor is the spinning part of a helicopter to which blades attach.

sensors—devices that tell pilots about the terrain and the location of objects in the air

special forces—troops trained in several kinds of warfare

TO LEARN MORE

AT THE LIBRARY

Alvarez, Carlos. *Army Night Stalkers*. Minneapolis, Minn.: Bellwether Media, 2010.

David, Jack. *United States Army*. Minneapolis, Minn.: Bellwether Media, 2008.

Kaelberer, Angie Peterson. *The U.S. Army Special Operations*. Mankato, Minn.: Capstone, 2005.

ON THE WEB

Learning more about military machines is as easy as 1, 2, 3.

1. Go to www.factsurfer.com.

2. Enter "military machines" into the search box.

3. Click the "Surf" button and you will see a list of related Web sites.

With factsurfer.com, finding more information is just a click away.

INDEX